The Lantern Bearers

The Lantern Bearers

ELIZABETH BURNS

*Alice —
with love,
Elizabeth*

Shoestring Press

All rights reserved. No part of this work covered by the copyright
hereon may be reproduced or used in any form by any means –
graphic, electronic, or mechanical, including copying, recording, taping,
or information storage and retrieval systems – without written
permission of the publisher.

Typeset and Printed by Q3 Print Project Management Ltd,
Loughborough, Leics
(01509) 213456

Published by Shoestring Press
19 Devonshire Avenue, Beeston, Nottingham, NG9 1BS
Telephone: (0115) 925 1827
www.shoestringpress.co.uk

First published 2007
© Copyright: Elizabeth Burns
ISBN-13: 978 1 904886 50 1

Shoestring Press gratefully acknowledges financial assistance from
Arts Council England

ACKNOWLEDGEMENTS

Some of these poems have been previously published in *Aireings, Brittle Star, Cencrastus, The Dark Horse, Images of Women* (Arrowhead, 2006), *Magma, Markings, Mslexia, Poetry News, Poetry Salzburg Review, Scintilla, Such Strange Joy* (iynx publishing, 2001), *The Thing that Mattered Most* (Black & White Publishing, 2006), *Zed 2 0*, and in the digital anthology *Watermark* (Flax Books, 2007).

Others have been published in pamphlet form by Galdragon Press as *The Time of Gold* (2000), *The Alteration* (2003) and *The Blue Flower* (2004).

CONTENTS

I – The Lantern Bearers

The lantern bearers	3
The curtain	4
Fields for my daughter	6
The bird Kezia	7
The time of gold	8
The secret	9
Creature	10

II – The Price of Light

The price of light	13
Sundial	14
The holly leaf	15
The alteration	16
Grandfather in the kitchen	17
Grandmother	18
The word	19
On holiday in Scotland, 1st July 1999	20
The return	21
Cathedral	22
A winter's tale	23
The moth trap	24
Making a landscape	25
Sea campion	26
First day in Amsterdam	27
A German fairytale	29
The miller	30
Preservation	31
A litany	33
Questions regarding the deaths of two Covenanter women at Wigtown in 1685	34
Returning the icons	36
Gifts	38
Painting the sea	40

III – The Blue Flower

Parcels for Gwen	43
Annunciation	44
Loving Chloë	45
The visitation	46
Talking to Fenella	47
The nun	49
The convalescent	50
The precious book	51
Girl praying	52
The path	54
The pilgrim	56
Interiors	57
Last letter to Dorelia	60

I – The Lantern Bearers

THE LANTERN BEARERS

Each November we watch them,
stumbling in the dark along the cobbled lane,
faces lit by the glow of nightlights
nestling in the homemade lanterns
that dangle from their mittened hands.
Carefully they carry the wavering flames,
clouds of breath rising in the frosty air
as small voices sing their lantern songs.
Hats down over ears, feet stout in boots,
there they go, marching into winter,
and in each of them – Tom, Maisie, Jess, Amy,
the line goes on – a quivering flame
carried in the still-translucent lantern
of a new-made body:
a fiery heart flaring up
then softening to embers,
or shining with a steady yellow light.
Look at them, tiny bright stars
coursing out into the darkness
that enfolds us all. And then, again,
they are ordinary children,
in a fumble of buttons, laces, stuck zips,
dripping wax, torn lanterns
as they crowd inside to the warmth
of homemade soup and chunks of treacle cake.
Later, curled up on laps,
they will listen to the story, told by candlelight,
one of the old tales that have always been told
at the onset of winter:
the story of a lantern bearer
setting out on a journey into icy dark
and, by the eye of this one candle,
finding the place at last,
its doorway glowing with light and fire.

THE CURTAIN

It was how we knew you'd be born at home
after all: when the waters broke and the midwife said,
You're going to need a curtain at that window,
for in the new and unused room there were only folds of muslin.
Someone found the cloth of bluish-purple silk,
hitched it up against the night sky
and the neighbours' eyes. We lit the lamp.
The room was dim and warm and smelt of lavender.

All that hot night long we wracked each other's
bodies, you and I, hours and hours of it,
and it must have been four or five in the morning
when I saw, through the tear in the makeshift curtain,
the sky begin to lighten, dawn coming, and they said to
push, and we pushed, and I fixed my eye
on that rent in the curtain, the crack
of lightening sky, moving from a violet-grey
towards soft blue, a way of knowing
that time was passing, that the day,
the day of your birth, was on its way –
and then it must have been sixish,
in the gash of sky the blue was deeper,
and how we pushed, you fumbling out through that
cloth of flesh, as though you were smothered in
velvets, looking for a chink of light, edging your way
towards it, and I, I was trying to get you there,
heaving you out, your matted head ripping through silk
and then the slither of your little body and I looked upon you
as your blue eyes gazed about you
at so much light.

*

A summer morning. A girlchild suckling.
A flurry of midwives clearing up. And only that slit
of light to show that it was well past dawn. Later,
when I saw the whole skyful, lit by the bright hot sun,
the blue so vast and raw, the light so fierce
after the night in the dim-lit room,
I blinked with the shock of it –

as if I had not seen a morning sky before,
as if love were a pool
I had only dipped a finger in
and now it drenched me in its blue –

*

We left the purplish curtain there, twisted it in daytime
into swathes, so that all those hot sleepy afternoons
as we dozed milkily, calm now, on clean sheets
and with the scent of lilies in the room,
the sun washed through shot-silk, stippling the walls
with colour, as if from stained glass,
and brushed your new skin, soft with vernix,
dappling you with lavender-coloured light.

FIELDS FOR MY DAUGHTER

'Make a field, make a field,' she says,
and we do, daily, out of the bricks her grandfather carved,
and they have gates and walls and fences
and animals enter them – the little wooden goat,
the elephant, sheep, giraffes, pigs, all lie down together,
lion and lamb, chicks and tiger –
and sometimes there are chimneys
(those tall blue bricks she likes)
and sometimes a wooden path will lead up to a field,
or there'll be a pond where the painted fish can swim.
Some fields hold treasure: glass beads
that glow like sapphires and rubies
heaped behind the barricades of bricks.

Outdoors, her fields contain leaves, petals, stones,
take on the semblance of nature.
On beaches they're made of pebbles, driftwood,
filled with shells and the feathers of gulls.

These safe havens: the fold of their walls,
the wildness of what grows in them.
I remember the meadow we walked through
the day of her first-birthday picnic,
brimming with wildflowers and butterflies,
and want to promise her a world of fields
like this: not a land of rape-seed, set-aside,
pesticides. Not those silent birdless fields
without hedgerows, without insects,
where chemicals trickle into river-water,
but fields like the ones we make together
where animals gather and graze
and the three-year-old girl from next door runs in,
stops in her tracks and exclaims:
'Oh what a beautiful field.'

THE BIRD KEZIA

From the moment I first
dreamed your name
I saw you as bird
a winged creature, set for flight

and then a fledgling
trapped in a chimney
little wings
beating the sooty walls –

until you were out of that darkness
stretching and curling
breathing and breathing
exploring the curious air –

THE TIME OF GOLD

It was a time of gold
– the rich light of autumn, ambered leaves,
orange pumpkins on the windowsill
burning like two harvest moons –

and I'd imagined for your birth
chrysanthemums, big ruffled petals
of yellow-gold and bronze

but the flowers they brought
were white and delicate
lightly perfuming the room:

the room where the pain
I'd imagined would go on all night
did not, so swiftly you slid
from your moorings

for it was barely dusk
when they cut the rope that tethered you
and you were swimming in air
your skin on my skin

and we wrapped you then in white
the warmed soft-cotton nightdress
and the muslin shawl

and when the lovely evening, candlelit, was over
we lay down on either side of you
and cradled you till morning

when the opened curtains
let in October sun
and plunged the white room
into gold.

THE SECRET

That the sweet honey of motherlove
is laced with a raw, sour fear
of loss, a fear whose smell
I live with now, knowing that the world
is heavy with it, the air
thick with the stench and ache of it

and I know too the other secret,
that underweaving everything
is the web of love that spins between
mothers and their children, this dark and delicate
net that loops us all, encloses us
and holds us fast.

CREATURE

New-made, skin thin as lantern-glass
that lets the light pour through,
you're still balanced between elements,
each one rich in you, and equal,
pulling like magnets. Your compass whirls.

The earth is where you live, it takes your shape
like a hare's, rolls you giddily down hills,
draws you to itself with mushroom smells
and orange leaves. You clamber over limestone,
stretch for blackberries, purple-fingered.

Wind takes you: you skitter like a kite,
touch clouds, full of bluster,
skim the ground like old blossom.
Winter mornings, cold douses your lungs.
Breath hangs in the mist.

The sun's your best friend, calls for you,
off out to play together. Staying up late
on summer evenings, your hoop turns to gold.
Night, and a candleflame shines back
from the iris of your eye. Fireworks crackle.

Sea-water's inside you: taste your salt tears.
Dip a toe in a rock pool, tumble into spray.
Fall asleep to the sound of the waves.
Cross the river on stepping stones,
set sail your boat into the world.

II – The Price of Light

THE PRICE OF LIGHT

'…deep surroundin' darkness
Is aye the price o' licht.'   *Hugh MacDiarmid*

Midwinter in the burial tomb: low sun
reaches in and marks the inner wall,
an amulet of sunshine in the darkest moment
of the winter, and in the place of death.

Slivers of brightness, sharpened by the dark:
a fallen crimson bauble underneath the tree,
its sudden gleam a huntsman's fire
blazing in the forest against the howl of wolves

or one scarlet leaf in the wet leathery heap,
jewel petals of anemones, beside a soot-black centre,
last red embers in the blackened stove,
and the lit wicks of our lives

flickering enough to illuminate a tomb,
its dark made bearable by any glimpse of light.

SUNDIAL

Stand with your feet on *January*
and the shadow you make will fall
on the carved-out clockface on the ground.
But at nine o'clock the sun can't rise
enough to reach here, though it's pouring
itself through the roofspace of the glasshouse

and here's a pale slant of light
on the frosty grass, just room enough
to show your shadow: no markings,
no device, simply these two planets
and your body caught between them
laying out its line of dark upon the earth.

THE HOLLY LEAF

The spider's web hooked in the holly tree
so exactly resembles the shape of a holly leaf

it's as if a leaf had been a template, the web
spun over its surface, and then the withered leaf,

no longer needed, fallen to the ground.
The web is a hammock, slung between twigs,

the thick-meshed floor of it almost opaque,
and swaying in the breeze, a tiny billowing,

held up by a rigging of threads: this ghost-leaf,
memory of leaf, sunlit and intricate,

the thing that remains in the tree, while the body,
the spiky body, falls to the ground and is mulch.

THE ALTERATION

At eighty-nine, her red hair has not whitened,
only grown lighter; as do the leaves
of the copper beech, the whole tree
losing its heavy shade of burnished bronze,
the almost leafless branches lifting in the air,
the leaves so pale before they fall.

GRANDFATHER IN THE KITCHEN

The memory of this has been distilled
until all that's left is whiteness –
the bleached wood of the stool
with the fingerhole to lift it,
the enamel surface of the table,
his cotton vest as he stands by the sink,
face in the mirror bearded with shaving soap,
the warm milk keeping on the stove.

GRANDMOTHER

carries the guid Scots tongue in her heid
all the way to London

where it becomes like the kitchen china
worn and cracked with use

kept in the press with the girdle and the spurtle,
the ashet and the jeelie pan.

The good china of English
is what you bring out for visitors:

kept in the credenza
with the key in its lock.

Lift it carefully onto the silver-plated tray.
Remember which language

you're speaking in. Dinnae –
Dinnae forget.

THE WORD

'There's your doolichter,' he says.
patting his granddaughter's baseball cap
and a new word enters our vocabulary,
each of us trying it out on our tongues,
a word locked up for so long
in my father's memory,
a word, he says, his father used,
a word now suddenly free,
spreading its wings again,
alighting on us all like a dove.

ON HOLIDAY IN SCOTLAND, 1ST JULY 1999

The day the parliament was opened
we were pottering on the beach
not thirty miles away, I and my daughters,
throwing pebbles into rockpools,
gathering shells and drawing on the sand

watching blue seawater
that had flowed down the Forth
and was moving on now, out into the open sea,
the North Sea, off towards the coasts of Europe
and all the while the wide Scottish sky
bent over us, full of its summer light.

The day the parliament was opened
was the day of the picnic, the boat trip,
the swim in the sea,
it was the day Maria came,
the day the wee one ate two icecreams,
the day of seals and puffins,
a day to write about on postcards,
a day to remember all your life

the day the parliament was opened
and was found to contain song and poetry
– things you want from a land.

Later, when we had gone back across the border,
it was enough just to touch the petals
of a white rose after rainfall

for the heart to crack like a mussel shell
crunched underfoot on hardened sand.

THE RETURN

For years you've held the memory of this place
delicately, like the shell of a bird's egg
cupped in your hands: a place of childhood,
sometimes glimpsed in little snapshots,
black and white, or felt in the sudden jolt
of what you remember – fingers in soft black earth,
a warm greenhouse smell of the stalks of tomatoes,
the gap in the hedge that led to the heath,
the church with its steeple and blue-painted door;
and the sea, and the path that you took to it,
down through the sandy-floored pinewood,
and then to come out of the dark smell of resin
and enter the glitter and sparkle of waves.

You're scared to revisit this harbour of memory,
scared of disturbing the silt – and yet here it is,
touched by your hands, and nothing is spoilt after all
when you visit the house by the heath,
when you see the waves sparkle, the way that the light,
sheer from the south, falls and refracts on them –
and the memories are a brimful glass of water
that you've carried so carefully over the years
to find by a miracle none of it spilt.

CATHEDRAL

Keep your eye on the white spire in the clear blue sky,
follow the river of willows and swans, skirt round
the watermeadows, and you're there and the cloisters
are cool in the shade; beyond them, in sunlight,
there's rosemary, and such bright forget-me-nots,
and blossom wafts perfume through archways
to where the clergy in their flapping robes
pace up and down. Inside, between the place of candles
lit once more for peace, and the wide blue window
for prisoners of conscience, stands the water sculpture:
font, pool, flat lake of water held still, almost overbrimming
its stone vessel, but the surface is constant, a black sheen
reflecting vaulted ceiling, stained glass, and barely moving
though there's water bubbling up and water curling down
into a spiral, water continually leaving and arriving,
keeping the vessel full, its liquid circle perfect;
and all around are coffins and their effigies, presences
of stonemasons and master carpenters, sounds of footsteps
shuffling on stone, voices of tour guides, murmurs of prayer,
the little girls tiptoeing and skipping, their great-uncle
moving slowly with his walking stick. Cathedral
holds them all, its eye of water watching and reflecting,
so many souls passing through, replenishing, replenishing.

A WINTER'S TALE

Out of the blue sky, a drift of white flakes
falling on your coatsleeve, on the old oakleaves,
so for a moment it seems as if it's snowing –
but these are flakes of ash, blown upwards in that plume
of mauvish smoke. Peer over the fence, and look,
deep down in the amphitheatre, where the sun in winter
never reaches, below the rows of frosted benches,
in that place of trampled mud that is the stage,
there's a bonfire: a fierce blaze, the logs beneath
burnt white already, and the gardener dragging
down the aisles dead undergrowth and withered branches.

You stand and watch, as though this were theatre too:
the sloping rows of whitened seats, the shock of fire
in this dank place, this pit of winter –
where, on a summer evening, Peaseblossom danced
in her muslin dress of sweet pea colours,
Titania in rose petals and blue velvet
lay on a bed of ivy, Puck tiptoed,
spilt the juice of wildflowers on eyelids,
a lantern was the moon, your daughter sat on your lap,
her first Shakespeare, her eyes shining,
and above you in the warm night sky the stars came out.

The smell of bonfire smoke is hovering
in the cold blue air. The flakes of ash
are turned as if by magic into snow.

THE MOTH TRAP

She spreads a white sheet on the grass,
shines the ultraviolet lamp on it
and moths gather – yellow underwing,
copper underwing, canary shouldered thorn.
Everyone crowds round: it's like some bizarre picnic
in the dark, the sheet our tablecloth.
Someone asks why they're drawn to the light

and she says no one knows, but maybe
they navigate by a constant distant light
like always having the moon on their left.
They flutter round us, land on skin and hair
or settle for a moment on the sheet:
dozens of moths, pulled out of darkness,
this lamp a tiny moon to guide them by.

MAKING A LANDSCAPE

No sloping shore, no gradual trailing waves:
the sand stops, sliced sharply, the way peat is cut,
and here's the sea, lapping up to it, deep,
like a river in spate, a curdle of waves
rubbing the baulked edge of sand. But sea
can't be contained like this, sea has dug channels,
carved out its own particular curves, sculpting
slopes and ridges; and the channels
edge their way inland where sand turns to mud,
grown over with grass and purslane,
with thick-leaved plants that can survive salt-water
when the sea at high tide rushes in from the bay
fast as a galloping horse, leaps the wall of sand,
swamps channels, covers grasses,
swills driftwood almost to the road;
and submerges completely the place
where the sand, before it falls away so steeply,
is studded with shells, pinks and whites
and the seaweeded green of cockleshells,
and between them the fine markings
which are the prints of seabirds' feet,
making an intricate landscape, almost a shoreline.

SEA-CAMPION

Only when you get it home
and set it in a glass of water
with the mouse-ear and the sorrel
do you notice something queer
about the flowers:
petals ragged and mis-shapen, asymmetrical
and oddly clustered,
the silk of flower-skin crumpled.

You remember seeing paintings
of wildflowers next to nuclear sites,
how they were mutated and deformed,
and think of where this campion grew:
on a low ledge of cliff at the edge of the bay
round the headland from the power-station
which empties its waters into the sea
eight times each day.

You remember how your daughter sat
and made in the sand little graves
'for mice,' she said, and decorated them
with shells and stones and flowerheads,
then made a smaller one,
'for mice who die as soon as they're born'
and a tinier one,
'for mice who die before they're even born'.

And you think how the tide will have risen now
and the water with its silent freight of poison
will have washed away the sand graves
and be reaching up now to the grass,
soaking into the sandy earth,
touching the tendrils of plants,
seeping its way up through the roots
and into the delicate spoiled flowers.

FIRST DAY IN AMSTERDAM

She is learning that the starry coins are Euros,
that breakfast can be cheese and ryebread,
that she herself is *zeven jaar*.

She is learning that a city can be laced through with canals,
that bicycles can get you anywhere,
that a house can have six flights of stairs

and that people hid in attic rooms like this;
that a family could survive for years,
that friends will bring you food

and enemies betray you. She only knows
that soldiers came, and took them,
she does not know yet where the girl

– the girl not much older than she is herself,
the girl who wrote a diary, look, here it is,
you can see it with you own eyes,

the tiny writing, the tartan cover –
was taken. Or that we can do such things
to one another. She is learning

that writing can be secret, potent,
though it may not save your life.
That not all children will survive a war.

Here in the city of frozen canals
and straight lines and hard graft
she is learning that an artist

may be mocked if people think the way you paint
is queer; that all your life you may be poor
and your paintings never sell until you're dead.

But she is learning too the lovely blues of irises,
the way that blossom on a peach tree
sings against a fresh spring sky

and those colours in the painting of a river
which, months later, she'll be reminded of
by the blur of greens and yellows in her dress.

A secret diary. A canvas
turned against the wall.
Things that seems invisible

may one day dazzle with their glare.
A child marked with a yellow star.
A man stoned out of town.

An attic room. Thickness of paint.
Canals under ice. Crocuses in flower.
The world is kind. The world is cruel.

A GERMAN FAIRYTALE

The crumbs they've laid down to lead themselves home
have vanished. They're lost in the forest.
And then, like a miracle, a house made of cake
and pink icing. Chimneys of marzipan, a pathway
pebbled with sugarplums. Delirious with hunger,
they break off eaves, gobble up shutters,
bite the doorknob. They don't even see
the fence made of gingerbread children,
their raisin mouths like blackened teeth,
their hollowed-out eyes and the bone-white
flakes of almonds stuck to their skulls.

Full of sweet promises, a woman persuades them inside
and feeds them on pancakes and milk.

Then locks up the boy in a cage.
The girl she'll keep and work to the bone.

The dark mouth of the oven shuts and opens,
licks its lips of fire.

There is a smell of burning sugar,
and something else, acrid and unfamiliar.

The gingerbread children are ash.
On the ground lie the hard burnt raisins of their eyes.

Smoke hangs over the forest.
The birds have fallen silent.

The child holds out a bone,
thin as a finger with the flesh gnawed off.

THE MILLER

Then the wolf went to the miller and said, 'Miller, sprinkle my paws with fine white flour.' The miller didn't want to do it. 'If you don't,' said the wolf, 'I'll eat you.' So the miller was afraid, and did it.
    'The Wolf and the Seven Goslings', *Tales from Grimm*

It's the wolf who's meant to scare you
in this tale, the wolf who makes the children
jolt and gasp and quiver on your lap,
who makes them clutch your clothes
in terrified excitement
as he sniffs out each gosling,
and 'swallowed them whole in his horrid haste'.

But the miller is the one who scares you more,
the human one, the one who 'was afraid, and did it'

the miller who colluded, who was only
doing his job, with the tools of his trade

who whitened the wolf's paws
who dyed the cloth to make the stars
who welded the metal to make the signs
who laid the tracks that took the trains
who closed the door of her shop to them
who barred the children from his school

and you know you might have been the one
who dusted the paws of the wolf
who disguised and covered him
even as someone else's children
were being swallowed up —

'And when at last the goslings were freed
they cried out, *The wolf is dead, the wolf is dead*
and danced round the pond in delight.'

But the miller's heart was heavy
and sank like a stone.

PRESERVATION

Take this fragment of a painting:
a woman sitting in her doorway, sewing
— just the suggestion of it, the way her head
is bent, her hand is lifted, the way she peers —
and see how the light falls onto her lap,
how it rubs at the curve of her worn wooden clog,
and at the buttery yellow of her sleeve

and see the flecks of white paint on her skin
— a smudge on her nose, at the back of her neck —
her flesh made bright as the sunbleached linen
of her apron and cap, their whiteness
set against the ox-blood colour of her cuff
as a white wall frames the terracotta shutter

and at her feet, the slate-blue step slips down
to meet pale ochre pavement tiles. Cobbles,
brickwork, latticed windowpanes, the cloudy sky:
all overlaid now by a crackled glaze on canvas.

Gaze on all this: then let it be wrapped up,
let the whole painting, the woman and her street,
be folded now in thick cloths, sealed in a box,
bundled and carried like a child, taken down
under the earth, into the caves
that spread their passageways like roots,
miles and miles of them, an intricate maze,
plenty of corners, plenty of dark secret
places in which to hide a painting
while the S.S. stride the streets,
looting what they want,
any art they fancy for the homeland.

But not this woman seated in her doorway
who will remain for years untouched by light.

And still the caves are filling up with people,
thousands of them, leaving their homes, entering
the underworld, led by pinpricks of lanterns
into the labyrinth of passages that will become their city.
Here they will grow pale-skinned and weak with rickets,
as they queue for loaves baked in the makeshift oven
whose smoke must not escape. Here they will sleep
on gritty floors, wrapped in the smell of themselves,
made silent with the weight of secrecy.

When liberation comes, they'll take mouthfuls of air,
rub hands over rough grass, stroke the back
of the lame horse in the field,
blink in the suddenness of sunlight.

The boxes will be taken back to galleries,
the pictures hung, and eyes will look again
at this fragment of a painting:
a woman in a doorway of a street in Delft,
her face bent over, making lace –

A LITANY

after Michael Longley

I cannot name for you all the wildflowers
of the Machars I saw in one day, but I can tell you
that among them were sea campion and spring squill,
herb robert, burnet rose and scarlet pimpernel,
speedwell, bluebell, bugle, cranesbill,
sea radish and birdsfoot trefoil, eyebright and thrift,
red campion and ramson, primrose and violet

and I can tell you that at the end of the rocky shore
in the cave of Ninian, bringer of Christianity
there were laid little wilted bunches of these flowers
along with crosses made of driftwood
tied with scraps of rope or fishing net,
and smooth pebbles left by pilgrims.

I cannot name for you all the women of that place
killed as witches or as covenanters, but I can tell you
that among them were Helen Moorhead and Jean Thomson,
Agnes Comenes and Agnes Clerk, Elspeth Thomson
    and Elspeth McEwen,
Margaret Clark, Margaret Wilson, Margaret Maclachlan,
Janet Dunn, Janet Corsone, Janet Callan, Janet McMurdoch,
Janet McKendrig and Janet McGowane

and I can tell you that perhaps a sister or a friend
of one of these accused slipped down Physgill Glen at dusk
and made her way to the cave, even then when pilgrimages
were banned, and made supplication to the saint
and brought for him a pebble and a handful of wildflowers
she'd gathered and whose names she knew by heart.

QUESTIONS REGARDING THE DEATHS OF TWO COVENANTER WOMEN AT WIGTOWN IN 1685

If you had been the one to pull the drowned boy
from the river, if fate had chosen you
to lift him from the muddied water
that filled his lungs so completely that no air
could enter them; if you had held his body
and seen what the river in spate had done to it,
would you have ordered wooden stakes to be set
deep in the silt of the Bladnoch river,
and would you have given orders that two women
be tied to them with ropes and left there while the tide came in?

If you had held the limp boy in your arms,
would you have stood and watched as the tide of the Solway
rose higher, covering over the marram grass and sea-thrift
whose flowers give a haze of pink to the wetlands?

And would you still have watched as the water reached up
and soaked the skirts of the women, and the older one,
who was nearing seventy, fainted in the icy water?

If it had been you who had tried to breathe life
into the boy's mouth, giving your own breath again and again,
would you have stood by as water drenched the cloak
of the young woman, crept up over her new breasts,
lapped at her chin and filled her mouth,
forcing it to cease its singing of the psalms;
would you have remained there looking out across the estuary
towards the hills of Cairnharrow and Carsluith?

And if you had been the one to lay your head
on the chest of the boy and feel it flat and unmoving,
would you have remained rooted to that spot on the riverbank
with its hawthorn blossom and its bluebells
and buds of wild roses twisted in the hedgerow?

Would you still have gazed up at the May sky,
thick with birdsong, while the waves of the Solway
laid themselves over the women, would it have been in you
to do this if you seen the life of a boy put out so quickly,
so completely, as if it were a roaring campfire
doused suddenly in water?

RETURNING THE ICONS

Winter is ending, the ice is cracking
under the boat as they carefully lift

the shrouded paintings onto the shore.
They've reached Siberia: a tiny island

where prisoners have lived, and monks,
each cradling in the lightless days

the glimmer of a memory, a liturgy,
a poem learned by heart.

She's carrying one of the icons
under her coat, as if to protect it

from cold, as if to keep it secret
as her father once did, smuggling

holy pictures out of the country
into safekeeping in his English church.

She remembers stories of babies in wartime
who stay in the womb for more than a year

until danger has passed, and she smoothes down her coat
and knows that beneath it, close to her skin

is her favourite Madonna and Child. And now,
in the white beginnings of spring

with the gulags all gone, the barbed wire
down, and fresh paint on the domes

so they gleam in the sun, the icons
are back from their exile:

and all through the Orthodox chants
the radiant haloes of saints

are stroked and blessed and kissed
and it seems in the candlelit dark

that all those hands and lips you see
are flickering with gold.

GIFTS

Imagine a parcel of light,
fragile as tattered silk,

white as the memory of tulips
against soft folds of voile,

given into your hands by a woman
in a waistcoat patched with velvets

a woman in a country not her own
who has made of this room a home

with a bowl of hyacinths on the sill,
a junkshop cloth on the table

on which are apples, biscuits,
a snowdrop in a glass

and as she bends down to the children
they open out like petals

as though she were the sun, rain, air
in whose presence things unfold –

*

Imagine the parcel of light
unwrapped, and see what spills from it:

the dream of a white room
with gathered pebbles by the hearth

the memory of a strip of sea
like a blue needle pointing to the north

or of another, younger woman
sitting on the sofa of a sunny café

handing you a book of poems
and a dress of raspberry-coloured silk

then leading you out to a garden
smelling of herbs and lavender

where, as rain begins to fall
on dusty earth, you say goodbye

and take with you the package
that contains the book, the frock

and the lightness passed to you
which seems so tangible

it's as if you could wrap it up in tissue
and let it be held by your fingers

and let it be carried within you,
a whispered, invisible gift –

PAINTING THE SEA

'Of course I haven't got to get it looking like the sea. It's my response to the sea that I want.' Julia Ball

In Micronesia the sailors' charts
are made of lashed-together stalks of cane
showing the winds and currents of the sea,
and cowrie shells are islands, threaded on;
the sea as latticework, the memory of its tides
fixed in an intricate pattern of sticks.

And the painter lays down her version
of the waves and swell, the rubbed horizon
with its layers of colour through which tiny flecks
of buried pigment glint and quicken,
catching a sense of the lightness, the heart's lilt
as you enter into that expectant landscape

with its sudden alteration in the light,
the whitening of the sky, its opening up
as you travel over hills to Monreith Bay
and see already in your mind the pink-streaked rocks,
the papery flowers of thrift beneath the cliffs,
and the sea itself, a paleness in the west –

and then you're facing something calm and limitless
that lets you stare for hours,
placed as you are in the littoral
inside the painting and beyond it,
between the burnished texture of the surface
and the wake of memories it trails.

III – The Blue Flower

Poems from the life and art of Gwen John

'She saw herself as a flower, a blue flower, growing high in the Alps with deep strong roots.' (Susan Chitty, *Gwen John*)

PARCELS FOR GWEN

Chloë sends English tea, furs for winter
and an eiderdown. She worries about the cold.
There's the book by André Gide, prayercards
and silk stockings, a cheque for ninety pounds.
And would she like an almond tree?
They're beautiful, and bloom so early.

From Ursula it's almost always clothes:
the grey silk blouse, the blue serge skirt,
a cerulean jacket, lengths of ribbon.
During the war, *The Times*. Then Chinese drawings,
the Cézanne book ('very precious') and a print,
'a little feast of colour'.

From Dorelia, once, a teaset which arrives
broken. From America, John Quinn
sends a camera – a patron's gift –
for making copies of her paintings
and her father goes on sending
all the photographs he's taken of himself.

ANNUNCIATION ('A Lady Reading')

I am painting myself
with the Virgin's face.
I am Mary, waiting for the angel —

The room is still, the red-checked curtain
falls across a corner of the table.
There is a spotted cushion on the chair

and a book — leatherbound, dark brown —
whose pages spread open in my fingers
like a fan, like wings.

The way that I have placed things
so precisely — a pencil on the table
the dark folds of my skirt —

and the way that brushes fondle into life
cherry-reds and olive-greens,
the mulberry colours of the dress I wear

— all this can make the spirit shift,
lightly and imperceptibly
the way that grains of sand

slip through an hourglass
so that even a room of checkered curtains
and a wicker chair is holy

and the woman who inhabits it
may paint herself as Mary
waiting and waiting for the angel —

LOVING CHLOË ('Portrait of Chloë Boughton-Leigh')

('Three weeks in Paris! Will you sit for me?')

There's buried treasure in you
I want to excavate:

I want to paint you the way Vermeer
painted women, to show you
still and silent in your blue-grey dress
holding a letter and your thoughts elsewhere.

I want to show your heavy gentle hands,
the thin line of your collarbone,
I want to paint the markings of your veins,
the flecks of white in your hazel eyes

and then, like Vermeer,
the tiny milky globes of pearls
and the gleam on the links of your necklace
bright as goldleaf

as Bronze-age torques or Roman amulets
discovered under earth.

THE VISITATION ('Girl Reading at the Window')

I

Between the black dress swooping down to the floor
and the dark shawl hung over the chair
falls the white lace curtain

Between two crows' wings
the feathers of a dove

II

The transfiguration of the body
by the fall of light

the lit skin of the white throat
the halo of burnished hair
the golden concentrating face

TALKING TO FENELLA ('Girl with Bare Shoulders', 'Nude Girl')

Fenella, I want to paint you naked:
scrawny neck, sloping shoulders
little hanging breasts.
I want to paint you as you are,

unadorned, without your finery.
A pendant drooping down is all I'll leave you
or else just this: white chemise,
black sash, black bow.

No headscarf or embroidered waistcoat,
no earrings, bracelets, playing cards.
Or did you hope I'd paint you as a gypsy,
the way the men do?

Remember how we met –
you sat on the floor telling fortunes,
all the lady artists giggling
offering up their palms to be read

and then we walked in the woods outside Paris
everyone staring and calling out
as your scarves blew in the wind
and your fake gold flashed in the sun.

I am painting your hooded grey-green eyes
that remind me of the Welsh sea of my childhood
and I have your gaunt face shadowed.
Am I cruel? Do I strip away too much?

Let's walk in the Luxembourg gardens again,
let me see you with your giddy shoes, your jingling tambourine –
The glances that fix on you there are not cold
like mine, but full of admiration. I turn away.

I have been painting you for months, Fenella:
it seems we'll never let each other go.
I want these portraits finished, I want them sold
and never in my sight again

but I know that certain things will haunt me –
the sallow colour of your skin, the way your collarbones
jut out, and the sadness in your red-rimmed eyes
I cannot paint away.

THE NUN ('Mère Poussepin')

Seven times I have painted her,
once for each room of the convent.
Seven times I've begun on her face,
the whites and creams and greys of the habit
and sometimes a Bible and flowers on the table.

She is long dead. I paint her portrait
from the engraving on a prayercard:
I know it as well as I know my own soul.
She seems to be smiling, but cover one half
of her face and she's distant and sad.

I pull on the habit the dressmaker made for me
and look at myself in the mirror.
I know exactly how the wide sleeves fall,
how the white of the headdress looks in the light.
I know how it feels to be in disguise.

How simple to dress like this daily
and abandon my muslins and silks,
how easy to lose all those colours
and give myself over completely
to two shades of white and a grey.

For years I have worked on these paintings,
making her over and over again,
entering into the life of the nun:
her face and her habit, the hands on the Bible,
the flowers on the table, my eyes on the prayercard.

I wear her cloth, I know the shape of her hands
and the bend of her arms, the slant of her nose
and the curve of her eyebrows, the brown of her eyes:
her bright eye and her sad eye as they watch me
trying to become what she is.

THE CONVALESCENT

Isobel, I am trying to paint you well again,
my brush strokes healing you
as they make for you this painting of a girl,

her fine-boned fingers holding a letter,
the line of her eyebrows, her dark hair
and the white chair, the flax blue

of her dress against her skin,
that flush in her cheeks that echoes
the pink of the teacup –

Isobel, I am painting you well again.
See how I have placed these lovely curves
of chairs and rounded table, cup and saucer:

they make a space around the girl, a good place
for her body, and the colours will be soft
for your tired eyes to look on.

I am painting you well, Isobel,
I'm remembering how it feels to emerge
out of illness, the body still tender

and how each object touched
– by fingers on letter-paper, lips on a cup –
feels new-made and fresh.

*

But Isobel, you were not convalescing
after all. I wanted you well,
I wanted perfection, but while I painted

you were dying. You never owned
the picture I had promised you.
It did not have the power to heal. Forgive me, Isobel –

THE PRECIOUS BOOK

So precious that she holds it in a white cloth,
not to let her fingers touch or stain
the cover; but more precious still
are the words she reads, that she's absorbing
from the book which is lifted from her lap

as though she will in a moment raise it
to her lips which are the same pinkish-red
as the cover and kiss it, the unmarked book
with its creamy paper and peculiar smell,
its pages and pages of undiscovered words –

GIRL PRAYING

She wants to paint me praying.
She folds my hands together
and positions me exactly,

what light there is just falling on my face,
then she relaxes the slope of my shoulders,
lets my dress fall loosely around me –

        *

She wants me praying. I think about swimming.
My hands make the same shape
held palm to palm, the fingers pointed,

set for the slow grace of breast stroke.
I can stand here for hours and dream I am swimming,
pushing the heavy water behind me,

swimming away from the weight of my life,
the womanhood pressing too close.
Here in the water I'm lithe as a boy,

nothing encumbers me, I kick away weeds,
I am pushing and pushing the water,
hardly breaking the surface –

I'm deft as a fish, moving downstream
to where sun falls through trees
and hovering over the water

is a haze of damselflies.
Suddenly I'm out of shadow,
hit by light. My eyes turn away

from the brightness, my sure strokes falter.
The icy water lets go its hold on me,
my bare arms are warm

in the dappling sun,
my fingers are opening
spread wide in the light —

*

I stand as she placed me
and watch how my dress
and the walls that surround me

become the river I've imagined,
blue-greens matted with brown,
flecked with a dark red like blood.

Only my flesh is pale —
my face, my neck, my cool dry hands
held still in a gesture of prayer.

THE PATH

I

The forms I paint grow heavier:
they are monumental, sculpted
weighted to the earth

but their colours become those of mist and air,
pearl-greys and blues,
faint pinks and chalky whites.

No longer the single moment of illumination,
the sunbeam falling on a woman's skin
and on the darkness that surrounds her

but to live one's whole life
– to paint the whole picture –
suffused with light.

I am treading a path out of darkness
and my room is myself:
the white interior is mine.

II 'Girl in Rose'

Flowers in a glass
lay shadows on her rosy dress.
The coral-pink line of her mouth

centres the picture:
stamen amidst petals
drawing bees towards itself.

III 'Girl Holding a Rose'

Out of the grey-brown folds of her dress
emerge her enormous hands,
holding a rose of that same colour

as her pale pink fingernails
and as the lid of a box laid by the window
with its white hint of daylight

reaching out into the room
whose space is hallowed
and enfolds her.

IV

I live with these young girls
for hours: they are patient
and still as dolls beneath my gaze

as I paint their placid bodies
and transfigure them. So we become
inhabitants of one another.

THE PILGRIM

That place of lightness, paler skin
beneath the ribbons fastened at her neck
is where birdsong catches in her throat
and mingles with remembered phrases of the Mass.

Even now, seated on this chair, weighted
by the painting, she feels such airiness,
as if somehow there were wings at her back
as if her cloak might lift and float –

She has walked for so long it is strange
to be still, to sit like this for hours,
her hands curved like moons in her lap
holding the beads of the rosary

that slip through her fingers like pebbles
and it seems now that this was the place
she wanted to reach, this room
with its quietude, and a palette whose colours

are those of the landscapes she's walked through:
shades of sand or loam for her dress
her cloak in the milky blues of sea and sky
stippled with lilac, its shadows like smoke

or the feathers of doves. She is stilled now,
that quiver of restlessness
hushed, and the wingshapes are folded
like hands made ready for prayer.

INTERIORS

I 'Girl Sewing at a Window'

The room is a Dutch interior,
all intricate pattern and detail:
wickerwork chair, hexagonal tiles
wallpaper, lace curtains

even, through the window, the mirror
inside the house across the courtyard;
and here, light catching the brim of a hat,
the rungs on the back of a chair.

Amid all this, I place
myself. My oval face is small,
its tone that of walls, floor, curtain.
It is my dress, my voluminous dress

whose huge black shape is in the foreground.
Into this dark curve, I pour myself,
becoming secret, hidden in its folds:
a raven spreading wide her wings.

Thick with lamp-black pigment,
the heft of my gown
obliterates detail. Inside it, I become
the room's dark ballast.

II 'A Corner of the Artist's Room in Paris (with Open Window)'

The walls and floor are plain, all pattern
painted out. My great black shadow,
like a buzzard's warning to its prey,
is gone.

A book laid open on the table,
a cloak draped on the chair
telling of absence and return.
The window open to the sky

as if for a bird to fly in and out,
leaving nothing in the room
but that slight quiver in the air,
a feather drifting to the floor.

III 'A Corner of the Artist's Room in Paris'

The window's closed, the gauzy curtain
drawn. Light filters onto yellow eaves,
white parasol, a glass of flowers,
the table with its beeswax shine.

I step away from this, I paint
my room without my body:
my presence here invisible
as birdsong in an orchard.

IV 'The Teapot'

I am ten years older.
I live in different rooms.
These are darker times.
The colours are sombre:

grey, ochre, umber,
the mottled brown of a thrush's breast,
the warm dark of shadows
like a nesting place.

In a roomful of angles and edges
the round table is spacious curve.
On it the plump teapot,
the ellipse of a cup.

It's at these points of curvature
– the spine of a book, the table's rim,
the jar containing paintbrushes –
that light fractures the gloom

glancing off each rounded form,
each thing that gives
a human presence to the room
as though, like fingerprints,

that touch of pure white pigment
could define and lightly mark
the self and her embodiment,
the things her hands have held.

V 'Interior (Rue Terre Neuve)'

Years have passed: I paint the room again
and everything is white
or else that soft greyish-brown
smudging into white

like cygnets' feathers becoming those of swans.
On the white table, faint shapes
of cloth and tray and teacups,
slightly silvered, ghostly.

You cannot see me for the whiteness
of the room, but the span of my wings
is wide, they catch the swoop of light
and I am here: this is my interior.

LAST LETTER TO DORELIA

Dorelia, I have come to Dieppe to be near the sea
Another war is beginning and I am weak and so weary

I wear the velvet cloak you made for me and think of you

Remember back at the beginning of the century
how we thought we'd walk to Rome?
That summer we made our way south
slept under the stars or in stables
for money made portraits or sang
lived on bread and grapes, washed in streams
carried our easels on our backs

Those intimate days of our twenties —
how close we were then, such companions

Sometimes, Dorelia, as I came here on the train
I thought I heard your laughter, or saw your face
as young as you were then —

In the autumn we came to Toulouse
and took rooms, and I painted you there
in the lamplight, your shadow vast
as though it were your life stretched out
before you, the ghost of your future
Your face so intent and eager
your faded dress, the pile of books
How much we read then, devouring ideas —
we thought we could paint the whole world

But how dark the paintings were, how dim our rooms

My colours now are pale and daylit
It seems I inhabit light, am floating in it
drifting out across the English channel
and into the Atlantic, back to Wales
and the barefoot beaches of my childhood

I wrap your velvet round me as I dream

At night through the open window
I hear the old waves breaking on the shore